AURUM

VOLUME 85

Sun Tracks

An American Indian Literary Series

SERIES EDITOR

Ofelia Zepeda

EDITORIAL COMMITTEE

Larry Evers

Joy Harjo

Geary Hobson

N. Scott Momaday

Irvin Morris

Simon J. Ortiz

Craig Santos Perez

Kate Shanley

Leslie Marmon Silko

Luci Tapahonso

AURUM

Poems
Santee Frazier

THE UNIVERSITY OF
ARIZONA PRESS

TUCSON

The University of Arizona Press
www.uapress.arizona.edu

ISBN-13: 978-0-8165-3962-8 (paper)

Cover design by Leigh McDonald

Publication of this book is made possible in part by the proceeds of a permanent endowment created with the assistance of a Challenge Grant from the National Endowment for the Humanities, a federal agency.

Library of Congress Cataloging-in-Publication Data
Names: Frazier, Santee, 1978– author.
Title: Aurum : poems / Santee Frazier.
Other titles: Sun tracks ; v. 85.
Description: Tucson : The University of Arizona Press, 2019 I Series: Sun tracks, an American Indian literary series ; volume 85
Identifiers: LCCN 2018057485 I ISBN 9780816539628 (pbk. : alk. paper)
Subjects: LCSH: Indians of North America—Poetry. I Oppression (Psychology)—Poetry. I LCGFT: Poetry.
Classification: LCC PS3606.R429 A6 2019 I DDC 811/.6—dc23 LC record available at https://lccn.loc.gov/2018057485

Printed in the United States of America
♾ This paper meets the requirements of ANSI/NISO Z39.48-1992 (Permanence of Paper).

for Randolph England

for James Hooper

for Willis Wapskineh

The nobodies: nobody's children, owners of nothing. The nobodies: the no ones, the nobodied, running like rabbits, dying through life, screwed every which way.

—EDUARDO GALEANO

CONTENTS

ACKNOWLEDGMENTS

Grateful acknowledgment is made to the editors of journals and magazines where poems first appeared: *Hunger Mountain–VFCA Journal for the Arts*, *Corresponding Voices*, *Prairie Schooner*, *Ploughshares*, and the *Florida Review*. Portions of the Mangled Creekbed serial were also published in *TC Cannon: At the Edge of America*.

This work was made possible through support from the Lannan Foundation, the School for Advanced Research, and the Native Arts and Cultures Foundation.

Many thanks also to Jennifer Foerster, Britta Anderson, Malena Morling, Karen Kramer, Sherwin Bitsui, Jon Davis, Ken White, Arthur Sze, David Treuer, Trevino Brings Plenty, and Adrian Quintanar.

Special recognition to Jameson Chas Banks, Micah Wesley, and Monty Little, whose visual language brought this work to completion.

AURUM

LACTIFICATION

Taught to gnaw, to take a switch across the arches,
a worming sort whose armpits smell like mustard.

Strike behind his ear, forearms lashed and etched,
a bulbous fist strung with muscle. Nose, misshapen,
fungal curds over a frown ribbed and chapped.

Nubbin that sounds like clavicle, pocked, a slurry
of vice, tally of kin. A breath or a smother that utters
moth wings sapped to kindling.
                                    From a world stricken

with slog and all manners of knifing. A scuttle of aurum,
a smattering of ochre between the chomps and fangs,
torqueing his wrists from shackle.
                                    A culling of melanin,
his skull ensconced in choir song—a tale of wiry locks,
hank of charred skin.

ORE BODY

The shine off the street reflects the coming bustle of dawn, of plastic and bolted steel, neon and industry caught in the asphalt. And as the grass sweats—the groan of machinery echoing off masonry—the dust rises, sewing itself in the fat of trees, shining the faces of men in the ditch under hard hats, shoveling dirt, whose language rolls the tongue of digging. The clank and song of Mimbres, a music hidden in the busting rock and soil. This ritual of sunrise, of shovel, and the gearing mechanisms of progress reminds me of a man in unlaced high-tops finger-painting a wall. Smearing gold into brick. His face shined like gunmetal, and when he sucked the gold from a paper bag, I knew his ritual had something to do with time travel, with brick, before mineral, polygon, the invention of wheel, story of flat, firing of clay. And now making my way through this city whose streets are named by numbers and minerals—the sunlight breaking the haze of dust and exhaust—I realize the oldest thing in this city is thirst.

LODE

In the mirror I see how your mouth made vowels
when you sang into a mug of lager.
                              Always in the misted
window light—a gush in the throat—some memory
under your wrinkled brow.
                        Not eggs in the grease.
Not flame under skillet, but glowered lips gripping the strike,
minnow-shine in the divots of your forehead—sunup shading
craggy, punched sheetrock—my cheek scraping the balding
linoleum, crumbs of bacon and black pepper under the rust
speckled stove.
                  Not the stereo blaring the trailer tin,
no "poor man's dollar" hollered to the pounding of biscuit dough,
the rain shaking window,
                        just a wild grimace in the dark.

In the evenings watching your hair bounce
                                    until all I could see
was the dark.
            And the swallows of flat beer numbed me to sleep.

Looking at our faces I realize this isn't much, that all I have to offer
is the sound of road in the inner ear.
                              Thinking of those days,
I imagine melting your records in the slow embers of the woodstove fire,
watching them burn to black smoke, but this isn't about anger.

It's about our faces, my daughter's too, as we stand here in the mirror,
chest to chest, me holding her, twitching and stiff as she brailles my lips—

the black of her pupil a marble burnished with womb, not yet etched
with dolor—it's about your head wrapped in gauze,
                                        face stitched
nose to cheekbone.

SUN PERCH

It is late, but outside the night is glowing with snow and streetlight, quiet
but for the growl and skid of the plows. Winter, Syracuse, where the feinting
snow fusses and scatters until it collapses roofs and power lines.

And now sitting in that gauzy light, nothing but the sounds of sleep, my son's
cub-like snore, I am reminded my childhood was spent in another city, alone,
a boy who knew evenings only by the gradual blackening behind buildings,
jar bugs pinging electric poles, from the street curb hearing the clink of dishes,
chuckles of supper. I remember a fish staring blankly from the center
of a round plate rimmed with almond-eyed bluebirds—wings extended,
mid-flap—the fish, perhaps lightly steamed, then wok-fried, charred
along the belly, fins crisped, mouth open from its last breath, fossilized
in a reduction of fish sauce and honey—next to the plate, a bowl of steamed rice.

I sat at the table waiting, not knowing how to eat the fish or rice with chopsticks,
smiling as best I could while in Vietnamese John explained that I lived three blocks
away, that I had been home alone for days. His father looked at me as he left the kitchen,
wearing the shirt of a machinist, "Paul" sewn in above the right pocket. Later, I would
learn he worked three jobs, and on his only day off, Sunday, after mass, he would drive
his family to some faraway lake outside the city, where they would reel in sun perch
and net them boatside. The smells of cooking oil and aromatics fading, John translated
for his mother who asked me to sleep over, and I said, no thank you, smiled, walked
home to whatever misfortune awaited in that dark house, where the plumbing was empty,

my bed a palette of blankets on the living room floor. I said no, not out of shame,
but because I wanted to lie down and remember how I'd used my fingers to scrape
flesh off bones—skin tearing with it—and how I trembled when asked to eat the eyes,
fins, and tail. I remember now, how in the throes of labor my wife looked at me,
how she gripped my hand when the pain ruptured up, and how through it all,
behind the brown webbing of her pupils, there was gentleness.

                                                When our son
finally came, he could not breathe, he was blue, motionless. I remember the midwife
rushing him off, and minutes later hearing gasping bawl. I didn't know what I saw,
as my son shivered, hands gnarled, locked in cry, still blind from birth, breathing
underneath a plastic dome.

                                  Thinking of it now—that faraway lake, my first catch flopping
in the boat, and later jerking the hook from its mouth—the perch must have stunned
at the sudden uselessness of its gills, and as I watched it gasp against the hull of the boat,
I wished what all boys wished for, a way of remembering how air rushes from your body
after being socked in the gut, and how to sit in the dark, alone, when streetlight is enough
for a boy to make shapes with his hands, a play made of light, light made of snow.

CHAAC

With nails like almonds
       he stirs the ropy strands.

Naming the gossip, clicking
       his tongue, spit whitening
the creases of his frowning lips.

Under his jaw a gobbler shaking
       to some erased syllable, the sound
of sapping or pecans unfastening
       from the limb.

Along the rim of the bowl
the paint is thinning to steel,
                       a vine
       of strawberries gnarling
into mounded leaves
he pulverizes between thumb
       and pointer.

Thirty-five years ago,
       a voice of poplar bark and mist
healed a misshapen tongue,

a tongue that sounded like river water
       slurring around a slick stone,

the way unthawed snow shapes
       itself into the skin of snakeroot.

And now, knife in one hand, potato
       in the other—
the curved blade slicking away the dirty
                         membrane—

a fog shreds
       the balding hillside.

SANGUINARIA

A bullwhip—handle wrapped
      with duct tape, the ends knotted
to halt the unweaving—
          a revolver
wrapped in a bandanna, a fillet knife,
      k-bar, a pair of brass knuckles—
flecks
      of blood in the dents.

Every Friday, after work, he parked
      the T-Bird underneath the shade.

I remember my toes
          gripping the limbs
watching as he unwrapped the pistol,
      cocked the hammer, squeezed the trigger,
loaded the shells.
          I remember the wind
dusting up the hillside, bending maple
      and oak, trailer windows latching
shut.

He liked the quiet of a ditch, the snap
of skull crushing into smaller snaps, the way
skin flays off the collarbone.

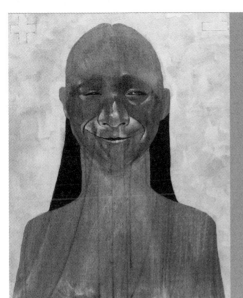

Skillet breath.

                 Tongue

                          sour,

wet with mash.

Dirt shackled,

                 clanking his bones

up the road.

MANGLED & THE ACCORDION

The cloud yonder frailing rain, Mangled sings "Kaw-Liga," playing his ribs, thumb to pinkie, pressing the flesh between bone, foot tamping pavement. Weaker than hay, small liver for innards, face shallow as wren's beak threaded into the blacktop, Mangled drags his boots, pinging rocks off fence posts on an evening fraught with diesel.

It's true, he sweats too much to hitchhike, the brim of his hat limp over his grease-shined mug. Strolling the wind-etched flat of Texas, through the dairy-dust-ups, hens murmuring through shack tin. Mangled, aimless till dark.

MANGLED & THE DEMON

Mangled liked to spin the chickens,
            how they danced headless
in the dirt, unable to cluck, flapping
            their wings in the tin shack.

He ate lunch outside the chicken house,
            white plumes stuck in his taco hat,
            eating boiled eggs and wild onions.

He smelt like livers, like chicken head,
            his skin dark as a plum.

And as he roamed the pasture, he saw the Demon
            on cinderblocks,
windows busted out, the hood propped up,
dirt-dauber nest in the muffler.
                      Mangled thought of tanks,
of spark plugs and pistons,
            and the crunch of steel.

TWICE-RUINED

Mangled does not remember the beating outside the tavern,
just that when he woke the air under the rumbling bridge smelt
like hot engine oil, like tire. His twice-ruined face inflated, cheeks
and hair crusted with muddy earth, boots spackled with blood.

Crouched near a creek, saw his face wavy in the ripple,
slit eyes buried under swollen flesh. He thought of the knife,
its baptism—flicker of sunlight on the current—blade hidden
behind the rust. As Mangled dipped his face in the water he saw
the creek bed, minnows darting along the moss-covered stones.

Mangled looked upon the distance,
      buzzards twisting above
the flung veil of sand.
                    No harvest he could see
in the wiry
        acacia, sinew
stretching to the nothingness of desert.

MANGLED & THE ACCORDION

Mangled in the knife-etched stall, hat tilted over his eyelids. The light blares him to sleep. In the dark of brain, he hears the knife, the hollow click of steel and bone in the palm. Hears the sound of skin flayed from an apple. When he mashes keys and squeezes, daylight tunnels to fuzz. Brailling the slick of ivory like the cue ball he cupped into the dome of the barkeep who poured him short.

Mangled playing songs of gutted stripers, of knife puncturing belly, of fish heads tossed in a bucket. Mashing the buttons as he sounds out the words "bone skeleton in the bucket fills." Tamping the tile, in the knife-etched stall.

THE SKEWERED FACE

Mangled skin cooked thick from slogging
through midday July, among the metal noise
     of work, flatbeds, trailers,

and eighteen-wheelers. Mangled the color
of fired clay, face like bark, eyes yellow
     as beer. At night he could hear the quiet,

the town sleeping in the buzz of light.
Clamor of mutts and rats in the blackness.
     He thought of LuLu's round face, pudgy,

the apple in front of it, the blade slung
through them both, her neck lank, the town
     folk hushed.

Lost in the city, he roamed the gridded
alleys, trudging toward signs he saw:
     TRUE LOVE'S, BIG RED, CRAZY HORSE,

THE FORGET IT. He made money sweeping
the planks, wiping down bar stools,
     mopping the bathroom. He slept

on a cot in a storeroom among kegs,
spent bottles, and vessels once
          anointed with fermentation. During open

hours he floated from shadow to shadow
bussing tables—butt-filter in the grit of his
          gums, in the grit where teeth once rooted.

Mangled reckoned at the bugs
     streaming up the fencepost,
         shine of their bodies that crunched
         between his fingers and teeth.
     He sat and looked upon the tilled pasture
tilted his hat and slept and dreamt.

MANGLED IN THE DEMOLITION DERBY

Mangled liked the way the car metal bent, how the engines
rumbled and the hazy night air stank of burnt tar,
       hamburger patties, and dumpsters.

A constellation of gum wrappers, cigarette butts, shards of glass,
grease monkey and a scatter of wrenches, and there out on the flat
       of Kansas, the gritty air under the stadium lights,
                                             Mangled
gripped the mop tighter, imagined his gloved fingers stretched
around the steering wheel, foot revving the motor, then launching
       himself into the red dirt arena amid the gaze and cheer of the grandstands.

MANGLED & THE ACCORDION

He forgot the sound of summons, the calling out at dusk when jar bugs blared
and deer ate—the thickening dark, leaves just sound in the dark, the dark the
way his breath felt as he mashed the innards, like the music of frying meat,
of squirrel thighs dredged in corn meal, the way Blue Rock's house smelt like
empty quarts of beers, acorns, and wild onion.

Music of lice wilting in kerosene,
of switch on skin—the wood still green and bendy.

MANGLED & THE ACCORDION

Mangled lights a match, his boots scuffed and frayed, lips gripping the cob-stem, strings of King Edward "Crimp Cut" glowing his face—a skillet shine, face of oily iron. No kin to call his own, the crunching of the box the sound of dirt-crusted ankles, of snoozing in a ditch, Mangled lips shine with slobber.

His fingers sound out the screen-door squeaking in the breeze, the crackle fire makes when the bark catches. The lung-sick box pinches Mangled's belly as he gnaws the cob-stem chuffing like a tailpipe. This is the end of his bit, calling down the knife, the slow dimming of his memory, crunching the box on the creek bank.

MANGLED & THE ACCORDION

It was not the accordion—keys still slick under his charred fingers—not his eyes foaming in the ducts. It was Mangled's tune, his humming of the knife, the slow slimming of his lips to song. His last fuss and bother in Terlingua. One of the steps of the old Chisos Theater, he squeezed the box, the strike half-lit, smoke churning out nostrils.

Knife in his teeth and accordion atop his head, elbows dipping into the current. Mangled slipped on the rocks. He let it dry in the sun, and when he played it by the fire, it buzzed with the thickened noise of critters.

MATINS

Outside the dusty town, the yonder is burnt orange. Sun still gnawing at the stars.

This is not fate the antiphon says, in this version of the tale you took to slaughter with
tawny chests fortified by the thin Andean air.

ORTHOS

Outside the dusty town, the yonder is burnt orange. Sun still gnawing at the stars.

This is not fate the psalm says, in the version of the tale you learned squalor
by sharpening your skull to solanum, by flaying skin with a fluted blade.

HALF-LIFE

In your grip,
            a lighter—
thumb and flint—
sparking to flame.

Blankets ablaze,
              the muted fire of fabric.

—

They leap a puddle,
　　　dome bellied—
　　　sticky with pop—
plum-dark feet and ankles.

—

Cranium crammed
                    through the windshield.
T-Bird bottomed-out
                    in a ditch—
dash still lit,
            a school of cans
                        scattered across the seat.

—

Television static,
    silhouette,
        his head bobbing
    like an oil derrick—
    hair a wiry frizz—
projected on the sheetrock.

—

You see morning sun yellow in splintered wood paneling,
        brass hands of clock blistering like rust.

Pinto beans,
         salt meat melted into the juice—
cornbread,
       mustard
yellowing the mash.

           Can-shaped meat,
                   sliced,
fried in bacon grease.

—

Twelve shots tipsy, the clack and stumble of boots.

You stuff balled-up socks between
the floor and door—
                    the drunk jams his foot.

—

Through almond-shaped mask holes,

                                    pulsating lips wet with snoring,

shirt off, jeans unbuttoned, work boot for pillow.

Gashed knuckles, burn-scar shaped like a three-pronged fork
on the round of his shoulder, cheeks cratered, nose shiny, fungal.

School of cans, ashtray spired orange—it is Halloween,
the trailer house lit dim blue, outside

                             leaves scatter

                                      applause.

—

Through almond-shaped mask holes you see a dim-lit bathroom,
small hexagon tiles,
                    black and white, patterned to shape
a walkway,
          the stalls boxed and beamed wood.

On your tippy toes, neck outstretched,
you see, projected on the mirror,
                              scribbled on a paper plate,
crosshatch of screech owl's face,
                              tied to your head with fishing twine.

With your finger find where crayon meets paper,
eye-holes cut jagged with a razor blade.

—

On your knees, swiveling on a stool,
scan your face in the neck of a whiskey bottle,

                        glowing in the amber.

It is Easter, your kin clacking billiards
gulping down pickled eggs and beer.

You stand at a pinball machine mashing the flippers—
the deep ding of steel

              the ball slicking its way across the plastic,
a carnival in a box

          like the sound of bees popping in a paper bag.

Projected on the back-glass, your face and Dolly's lit up
like gospel, hoot and stomp, echo in the tavern. The juke
bright against the cinderblock, "THE FORGET IT"

                     —blinking. Pink. Neon.

—

Iron glowing in the dim—the trailer house skewered by smoke pipe—
walls smeared by greased-up hands,
                              sink overflowing with crusty pans.

Your ear to the floor, you hear cars shadowing a scene on curtains—
        chrome and glass shaking the trailer tin.

Ear to the floor one eye in the crack of the door you see a curling iron,
        empty pack of Kools, bits of crumb and toenail
        hardened pools of wax, red as lovemaking—the smell of mucus and salt.

—

Nomads in the city peddling jailhouse scrawls of silver and gold wigwams.

You hear the factory
jutting and jogging
cans of corn niblets
down
a snaking ring of bearings.

—

Can in the fist,
he showers the aurum,

watches the blistered brass
clock hands strike
the minutes by slipping
a stripped gear.
          The dull tick of veneer.
Scrawls yardbirds in his ledger.

When the brick glows blue
bright,
      the night
slashing concrete
swallowing up store innards.

              RED OAK,

RED OAK,
      RED OAK,

blinking atop
the shingles—
      squalid

against a plywood roof,
Baptist spire lit
                dim and muggy.

Snap of wing,
               snap of exoskeleton,
the town sleeps
               to the falling creek.

When the dawn comes down
what rotgut will be chugged
where vomiting is concerned?
A grunt in the echo of latrine?

The carwash
               blue as mist,
blue as TV—
               shadow of mist—
his deadeye glowing
white
        in the socket.

Grunting his face
               in the puddle
can clutched—
            praying,
in the puddle singing
               his innards loose

in the stockyard—

                  where grass gnarls

a carburetor

           half-

               wrenched

from an eggshell junker.

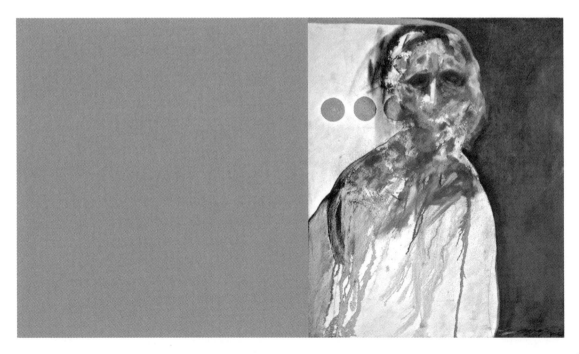

—

A sack to his grill.
Ventilator uncrunched lips
to spectacle—knuckles
canaled with aurum.

No face in the dime shine
of can.
       No face in the puddle
under the fluorescent awning
of SUPER S—
             fried burritos glowing
orange grease on a storefront
window.
       Gnashing his elbows
atop his hips—hugging himself
too blanked
          to arrest—
          kidneys boiling
in Night Train.

The path of pebbles
that makes road,
            the rain

crunching the can,
                    rain,
thumping his jacket
                    rain
eating the dust,
                    rain and road.

Hawking at the bits in his pockets,
tooth scraping grime from his nails.

You find his head jammed
into the crease
                    of a dually.

—

Yonder the far-flung pint
huddled in flies.

Amalgam of lip spit,
                              corn shine.

Long gone
                  the dim glow,
slit eyes,
            clamant mask,
carved by sun
                  and pucker.

Moss hair,
                  hide-veined fingertip,
joyous empty jaw.
                        Mangled
and blanked-out
                  hinging
his bones,
            clogging
a lark-like summons.
                        A stomp,

a barefoot trounce
                        on musky weeds.

Rail track slumber,
                        tar rock pillow—
smoldered turn in his coat.

Bean-scum
             face
dark as an engine,
lungs a freight whining steel.

Gold-speckled neck,
                      on the rail
rolling head.

—

                             Pickups bucking wing nuts,
                  carburetors,
distributer caps,
            or dislodged earth.

—

The radio whispers
a piano that vibrates
                              gospel
when it utters.

Simmering corn filling the house
with a nutty perfume.

What sounds but guzzle
of a pumped well
the gushing water against metal?

This is slowness,
                              scything of grass,
chucking grain toward
chickens,
               low barks of hounds.

Gnats backlit by the sun,
                              their flight pattern
scattered in aurum.

Song of exoskeleton,
zoom of the june bug's wings—

                   lifting itself

from the screen door,
off into the damp night.

Faraway roar
          of tire,
bucking junk in the truck bed.

Slow sputter and buzz
of a mower, echoed in the gully.

The woodstove in the dark.
Its bulbous hull

          a womb

               of popping embers.

—

Standing in front of a pay phone.

Picks up the receiver,
                              dials
hangs up.

Dust-caked ankles, legs chalk brown.

Pain long gone from a gaunt face,
          streaks of tears parting the dirt and snot
on his bare chest—a whole boy naked,
          but for his sagging underwear. Arms strung
with muscle, a frowned lipping
of name into the receiver.

Against the post of the phone,
knees together, toes gripping the sidewalk,
          waiting for guts of metal to ding.
In some kind of trouble, breathing the carpet
crumbs, bruised remnants of clutches
from shoulder to face,
                              forehead lumped up
where knuckles struck,

his face rung,
knees buckled.
See a dawn-lit house
when the shrugs and pitch of sleep told him
to scout his own food in the half-hinged icebox.

When groans of vice sent him to the phone
with emergency,
not knowing what numbers
to punch, what things to say on the street corner,
when cars rev, engines rumble deep.

—

The grain makes everything smell fried.
Trains. All night. Stopping at the silos.
This is industry. This is sleep. The crust
in your eyes as you sing to the dew-slick
dandelions. It is a bowl of beans smashed
with mustard.
    You are peeling a scab
from your elbow—jeans holing at the knee.

The bus bobs your head against the glass,
your face dissolving against the diesels
convoying out of town.

—

Limbo your head
                    into the desk,
hear their vowels echoing
                    off the carbon steel.

This is the afterworld, the hoisting of feed sacks
into the truck bed, sawing of ribs in the slaughterhouse.
Snuff spit in a coffee can.
                        This is where you will be, jeans
holing at the knee.

This is not fate the textbook says,
in this version of the tale
                        you are to be crucified
or burned.

Rotors twisted wood to shreds.
You stare at the tip of a pencil,
                          light a mirror
on sharpened lead.

—

Next slide: "Old Chief Wooden Head Hatchets Down Kin." You stare at the fraying tip of
your shoe, your dome in the shine of light, the trooper's eyes glowing sapphire in the

sockets.

—

Outside the dusty town, the yonder is burnt orange. Sun gnawing at the stars.

This is not fate, the textbook says, in this version of the tale you ate the glacier.
Horses did not survive the bridge.
                              You are the slide on the wall,
model of the human skeleton.

—

Next slide: "49ers Chain Indians to Trough." You think of her knotted knuckles wrapped around a potato, shucking eyes from flesh.

—

Outside the dusty town, the yonder is burnt orange. Sun still gnawing at the stars.

This is not fate the textbook says, your village was razed, grunts smothered,
    children left to twirl legless in scorched maize.

ABOUT THE AUTHOR

SANTEE FRAZIER received his BFA from the Institute of American Indian Arts and his MFA from Syracuse University. Frazier is director of the Institute of American Indian Arts Low Residency MFA program. He is a member of the Cherokee Nation of Oklahoma. He has received fellowships from the Lannan Foundation, the School for Advanced Research, and the Native Arts and Cultures Foundation. He has published one collection of poems, *Dark Thirty*. Frazier's poems have appeared in *Ontario Review*, *American Poet*, and *Prairie Schooner*, among others.